Holy Water

Its Origin, Symbolism and Use

By

Very Rev. P. Canon McKenna, P.P., V.F.

"Thou wilt sprinkle me (O Lord) with hyssop, and I shall be cleaned, thou wilt wash me, and I shall become whiter than snow." – Ps. 50

Original Foreword

In offering this booklet to the public the writer is keenly conscious of its many defects. He does not pretend to have made deep research nor extensive reading in its preparation for the press. Indeed it is only a reproduction, or rather an expansion, of a lecture put together at odd times and places during brief intervals of leisure snatched from a busy missionary life. The lecture – delivered in Church – was the outcome of a request made by some members of the congregation who had developed an anxiety to know something of the meaning and history of Holy Water.

The writer desires to thank a few clerical friends who kindly supplied him with some of the quotations and anecdotes, and helped him otherwise in the composition of the little work.

P. McK.

The Author desires it to be understood that unless where he expressly states that the Church or the Holy See has recognized the truth of miracles or other supernatural manifestations referred to in the following pages he claims no credence for them beyond what the available historical evidence may warrant.

Permissu Ordinarii.
Dioec. Dublinen.[1]

---

[1][Editor: The original text is present with only minor changes to punctuation, footnote numbering and language. Citations are left unchanged from the original.]

Holy Water.

Its Origin, Symbolism and Use.

---

*"Thou wilt sprinkle me (O Lord) with hyssop, and I shall be
cleansed, Thou wilt wash me, and I shall become whiter than
snow." Ps. 50*

There is scarcely any usage or ceremony of such frequent
occurrence in the Catholic Church as that of sprinkling ourselves
or being sprinkled with Holy Water. We sprinkle ourselves on
entering our churches, and in our homes when rising in the
morning, and again when retiring to rest at night. We are sprinkled
by the priest at the principal Mass on Sundays. Holy Water is
sprinkled when we receive the Sacraments outside the church, and
almost in all the blessings which are given by a priest or bishop
inside or outside the church. In one of its several forms Holy Water
is poured on our heads at Baptism — our spiritual birth. The
sprinkling of Holy Water accompanies the last sad rites of religion
over our mortal remains; and the grave in which we are laid to rest
is consecrated by its hallowed drops. Yet it is a ceremony which is
but little understood — a custom of which the origin and meaning
seem to be unknown to the majority of the faithful.

What is the origin of this ceremony, what its significance,
what its benefit?

HOLY WATER

Ancient Holy Water Fonts

A traveler on the continent of Europe, especially in Italy, cannot fail to observe in front of some of the most ancient of our churches, viz., St. Ambrogio in Milan, St. Cecilia in Trastevere, St. Clemente in Rome, etc., etc., an open court or enclosure (*Atrium*). In the midst of this enclosure is seen a disused fountain surrounded by a stone basin. In the days of the early Christian Church, the fountain supplied water to the basin in which the faithful were required, by custom or rubric, to wash their hands and faces before entering the sacred edifice. The *Atrium* of the great Church built at Tyre, about A.D. 315, contained, according to the historian Eusebius, a fountain, erected by Paulinus, for the purification of the worshipers as they entered. Eusebius writes of such fountains as "symbols of holy expiation."[2] The basin surrounding the fountain is known in the architectural language as the *Cantharus*,[3] (κανθαρος). These holy fonts were sometimes elaborately finished, and had engraved upon them inscriptions of a religious character. The famous church of the *Holy Wisdom (Sancta Sophia),* in Constantinople, formerly one of the most magnificent in the Christian world – but now alas desecrated and used as a Turkish Mosque – has carved on its holy water font a Greek inscription which reads the same backwards and forward,

"ΝΙΨΟΝ ΑΝΟΜΗΜΑΤΑ ΜΗ ΜΟΝΑΝ ΟΨΙΝ."

---

[2]Euseb., *Hist. Eccles.* L. 10, Cap. 4.

[3]Specimens of the ancient *Cantharus* or Holy Water Font, dating from a very early Christian age, may be seen and are still in use at Mount Athos, Djebeil, Syria, and at Haja-Napa, Island of Cyprus. Boldetti and De Rossi mention several Holy Water Fonts as having been found in the Catacombs of Rome. The museums of Europe also contain many curious Holy Water Fonts of very ancient pattern. Taken from the *Catholic Encyclopedia*, 1910.

which means, "wash your consciences and not merely your countenances"; and St. John Chrysostom 2 (about A.D. 350)[4], reprimands those who, on entering the church, wash their hands and not their hearts.

In the above and similar inscriptions, and in the historical references given, we find a clue to the mystery of the old time custom which is the subject of this paper.

Symbolic Meaning of Holy Water.[5]

What was the meaning of this washing of the hands and faces by the congregation as they entered the church? Sometimes it was only a sprinkling. Surely it was not merely an external cleansing of the body, such as takes place private at home, or publicly in the baths. No. It was an external expression of profound respect for the Most Holy Eucharist which, in these far away ages, was places by the priest in the right hand of each communicant. The Holy Communion was then placed on the tongue, and so received by the communicant himself or herself. "When you approach to communicate," writes St. Cyril (fourth century), "let your left hand support your right hand which is to hold so great a King, and receive the Body of Jesus Christ in the hollow of that hand, saying, Amen."[6]

The awe and reverence with which the devout faithful of

---

[4]St. Chrys., *Hom. In Joan.*, 71.

[5]There is no doubt that the Apostolic Constitutions refer to the ceremonial ablution rather than to domestic washing (VII. 32) in the words .... Πας πιστὸς ἢ πιστὴ ἔωθεν ἀναστάντες ἐξ ὕπνου πρὸ το ἔργον ἐπιτελέσαι νιψάμενοι προσευχέσθωσαν.... *Let every Christian man and woman wash before prayer after having risen in the morning from sleep to undertake the day's work.*

[6]Cyril *Catech. Mystg.* V., pp 331-2.

the early Church regarded the Blessed Eucharist suggested to them this preparatory purification. Hence St. Jerome (fourth century) writes, "let the hand be clean that holds, and the heart be pure that receives the Sacred Body of Christ."[7] Wherefore the Church, from the beginning, attached a symbolical signification to this ablution of the hands and face. It was meant to be a type and symbol of a clean conscience and a pure heart.

The faithful of the first era of Christianity could have no difficulty in attaching a moral and mystic signification to the Holy Water font placed near the entrance of their churches. They were converts from Paganism or Judaism, and most of these converts were quite familiar with the symbolic ablutions and purification by water which were of constant occurrence in the religious rites formerly practiced among them.

Virgil, Ovid, Tacitus, Cicero, and other pagan writers make mention of such ablutions and sprinkling with sacred water, as observed by the heathens in their religious worship, a custom probably borrowed from the Hebrews.[8] So also an established custom among the ancient people of God was the ceremonial ablution and sprinkling with water, as we learn from the 19th Chapter of the Book of Numbers.[9] This sprinkling, as prescribed in

---

[7] Jerom., T. VII., *Com. In Ep. Ad. Tit.*

[8] Protestants who imagine that sprinkling oneself with Holy Water is superstitious, and, therefore, opposed to true religion on the ground that the pagans practiced a similar sprinkling should also maintain, in order to be consistent, that it is wrong for us, and superstitious to genuflect, to bow our heads or prostrate ourselves in prayer because the pagans did the same.

[9] In the open court by the chief entrance to the Temple of Jerusalem there was a large and handsome stone basin filled with clean water in which the priests and people washed their hands and faces before they entered the sacred building to offer sacrifice to God.

the Old Testament by Almighty God, did not evidently effect a cleansing from sin, much less was it meant to be merely a natural physical washing. It was simply a mystic purification, symbolizing the interior and spiritual cleanliness which should characterize those taking part in the worship and service of God. For instance, those who came into contact with a dead body, even whilst performing the religious rites of burial, were declared by the ancient law of God to be corporally unclean. Such persons had to be sprinkled with water, as well as their homes and furniture, and then were considered to be legally and exteriorly purified. The symbolical significance of ablution by water is seen also in the religious crusade of St. John Baptist. He baptized in the River Jordan all who came to hear him preach, and proclaim the advent of Christ. This was not a sacramental baptism which purified the soul. It was simply a sacred rite which disposed men for Christian baptism. It was an external washing which typified an internal cleansing of the soul. It imparted no grace or sanctification. It was a sign, a reminder to the people of the need of being purified from the defilement of sin. May we not see a similar symbolism in the action of our Divine Savior when He washed the feet of His disciples, as He was about to institute the Blessed Eucharist, and give them Holy Communion on the eve of His crucifixion?

Holy Water in the Early Church.

The references, which we find in the writings and discourses of the Fathers of the early Christian ages, to Holy Water, confirm our belief that it was used in the ceremonial of the Church from the beginning. St. Justin, Martyr (A.D. 163), informs us that in his time the faithful, in their assemblies, were sprinkled with water every Sunday. Similarly we have made mention of Holy Water by St. Cyprian (third century), and St. Basil (fourth century). St. Paulinus in his Epistle to Severus writes (fourth century), "Sancta nitens famulis interfuit atria lymphis Cantharus, intrantiumque manus lavat," (*i.e.*) the waters of the Sacred

Cantharus (font), in the atrium, serve to purify the hands of those entering the church.

Mention is also made of Holy Water or *Aqua Lustralis* by St. Epiphanius[10] and Theodoret[11] (both fourth century), and by St. Gregory of Tours[12] (sixth century).

Forms of blessing water and oil may be seen in the recently discovered *Pontifical* of Serapion, Bishop of Thmuis (fourth century), and in *Testamentum Domini,* an interesting Syriac manuscript of the fifth or sixth century also lately discovered.

St. Jerome (fifth century), and St. Gregory the Great (sixth century), likewise give testimony in their writings to use of Holy Water in their day. So also do St. Chrysostom[13] (fourth century) and Eusebius Caesar.[14] Perhaps the most striking evidence of the ceremonial use of Holy Water in the age succeeding that of the Apostles is found in Tertullian's treatise on prayer (second century). We give a free rendering of his words. "To what purpose are the *hands washed before prayer,* whilst the defilement of sin still adheres to the soul?" "The hands are really clean when they have not been employed as instruments of the soul to do sinful deeds. Many persons act superstitiously in this regard, inasmuch as they never begin prayer until they have *washed their hands*, even though they have just come from washing their whole body. If the hands have been participants in sin, let them, indeed, be washed, otherwise they have no real need of being washed." Tertullian adds

---

[10]*Contra Haeres. I. XXX.*

[11]*Hist Eccles. V. XXI.*

[12]*De gloria Confess. C 82.*

[13]*Homil 3 in Ep ad Ephes.*

[14]Serm. 51 and 229 in append.

that those who *wash their hands*, and not their souls, are like Pilate.

At what period the Church introduced the ceremony of blessing the water with salt, as we do now, it is very difficult to determine. Some writers have stated that there is scarcely any well authenticated mention of *blessed water* in the writings of the Fathers of the first five or six centuries. This statement is erroneous, for as we have shown, there are numerous references in the writings of that period to the *aqua australis, (i.e.)* expiatory water, purifying water, cleansing water. Synesius,[15] and ancient writer, refers to it as *aqua australis*, placed at the Church door for the expiation of the people. By this the writers of the time did not mean the water employed for Baptism, as is clear from the contexts. They meant distinctly the water which was placed at the entrance to the church. We have, besides, good authority for the statement that the water in the Cantharus was blessed from the earliest times,[16] so as to impress upon the minds of the faithful the significance of the ceremony of the ablutions or sprinkling at the entrance of the church.

Fornici,[17] a distinguished liturgical writer, states that the introduction of Holy Water is attributed by Marcellius Columna to the Apostle St. Matthew, whose action was approved and adopted by the other apostles, and soon became general. The same writer asserts (*loco. cito.*), that Pope St. Alexander I, who governed the Church, A.D. 109-119, and was the fifth Pope in succession to St. Peter, mentions in his decrees the ceremony of blessing water in

---

[15]Ep. 121.

[16]"Ejusmodi lavacri loco successi, ut aqua sacerdoti precibus benedicta... in ipso ingressu ecclesiae poneratur, qua... adeuntes... aspergentur." Baronius. Ann. T.I. 346.

[17]*Institut. Liturgic. Edit. Monasier.*, 1853, p. 388

these words, "We bless for the use of the people water mixed with salt, so that all who are sprinkled with it may be sanctified and purified by it, and we command this (blessing of water) to be done by all priests."

Fornici is not alone in supplying this evidence as to the antiquity of Holy Water. Durandus as well as the ninth lesson of the Office of St. Alexander (3rd May) testifies to the authenticity of the above quotation from the decrees of the said Pope.[18] Manifestly, then, the ceremony of blessing water must have been in existence already for some time, as we must infer from the above words of the Pope, "We bless," (*i.e.*) we are accustomed to bless water, etc., and the Pope then commands priests to continue the custom which seems to have been neglected or observed only by some.

Moreover, the very formula employed in the blessing of the water has come down to us from the first ages of the Church, and may still be seen in the Apostolic Constitutions.[19] The following are the words prefixed to the formula in question as given in the Apostolic Constitutions, "that it (*viz.*, Holy Water) may have the power to give health, to prevent or expel diseases, to put demons[20] to flight, etc."

---

[18]The decree above mentioned is also found in *Migne's* Greek Patrology, Vol. v., in the Annals of *Baronius*, in *Darras'* History of the Church, Vol I., in the *Petits Bollandistes* (Ed. Bloud, Paris, Vol. v., p. 297), and in Acta Sanctorum, May 3rd.

[19]VIII. 28, Ed. Legarde.

[20]This latter effect probably gave rise to the ancient and well known sentiment, *viz.*, that the devil hates Holy Water, or "I love him as the devil loves Holy Water," which, of course, is irony.

HOLY WATER

Shape and Position of Holy Water Font Altered in Course of Time.

In the course of time (sixth century), the Church abolished the custom – which was a disciplinary one – of having the Blessed Eucharist given into the hand of the communicant, and in consequence the ablutions at the font became less necessary. The basins diminished in size, and eventually disappeared from ecclesiastical architecture, giving place to the Holy Water stoups of more modern times.[21]

At first the Holy Water stoups were fixed in the masonry on the outside[22] wall of the church to the right or left of the main entrance. Later on they were placed on the inside near the door, perhaps for the purpose of greater cleanliness.

In many Churches, particularly in Italy, the Holy Water stoup is a detached basin of stone or marble supported by a pedestal or held in the hands of a statue, generally the figure of an angel. Its position is usually a little to the right or left of the main entrance, and on the inside. In some cases the stoup is an artistically decorated object bearing a scroll with the Latin words, "Asperges me, Domine, hyssop et mandabor, etc." The inscription is also done in the vernacular in several instances.

The bowl of some of these stoups is sufficiently large to allow a dozen persons or so to take Holy Water together. With the water in the stoups the faithful are accustomed to sprinkle

---

[21]In some churches the strange custom prevailed in the middle ages of having one Holy Water Font for the exclusive use of the clergy, nobility and gentry, and another for the use of the peasantry and poorer people. *Catholic Encyclop.*, 1910.

[22]In many of the old church ruins in Ireland and England the Holy Water Stoup may still be seen on the outside. The writer discovered one such in an interesting little ruined church (10th cent.) in Stradbally, Co. Kerry.

themselves, making at the same time the Sign of the Cross upon themselves.[23]

Holy Water – Ireland

A feature of the Church in Ireland, ever since the introduction of Christianity into this island, is the use of Holy Water with a strong belief in its supernatural efficacy. Students of Patrician literature are aware of the frequency with which mention is made of Holy Water in the scanty records that remain to us from the period referred to. The well known incident of St. Patrick and Dáire, mentioned in the famous Tripartite Life, is very much to the point. "*Uisce urnaigte,*" *aqua sancta*, is mentioned "in the story of Patrick blessing water, which then sprinkled over the dead bodies of Dáire and his horses brings them back to life."[24] "One day, Dáire's two horses were brought to him into his church. ...Patrick was enraged against them. The horses were dead at once... Dáire was wroth... A sudden cholic came to Dáire... so that death was nigh unto him... The wife [of Dáire]... sent to ask Patrick for Holy Water (lit. water of prayer) for Dáire... Patrick blessed the water and gave it to the servants, and ordered them to put [sprinkle] it over the horses and Dáire." "Thus they did, and Dáire and his horses arose at once out of death."[25]

Another very valuable authority on the use of Holy Water

---

[23]By a Brief of Pope Pius IX., dated March 23rd, 1866, an Indulgence of 100 days may be gained by sprinkling oneself with Holy Water whilst making the Sign of the Cross.

[24]*Tripartite Life of St. Patrick*, Ed. W. Stokes, Vol. I, Introduct. p. cxciv.

[25]*Tripartite Life of St. Patrick*, Vol. I, Introduct. pp. 228, 231, Edit. Stokes, Notes by Muichu, Maccu, Machtheni, Book of Armagh, fol. 6, b. 2.

in the early days of Christianity in Ireland is St. Adamant's Life of *St. Columba,* A.D. 600.

"Six men...whom he found...at the point of death, on being sprinted by...Silnanus with the *Water of Benediction*, were...cured that very day. The rumor of this rapid cure spread throughout all the district devastated by that pestilential disease, and summoned all the sick people to St. Columba's legate, and he, according to the Saint's command, sprinkled men and cattle with *water*...and the men forthwith recovered full health and were saved with their cattle, and they praised Christ in St. Columba with heartfelt thanksgiving."[26]

"Let the...*Blessed Water* be poured upon her...and immediately on the name of God being invoked...the holy virgin will recover perfect health. As soon as Lugaid came to the holy virgin...she was [aspersed] bathed with the *Blessed Water* as the Saint [Columba] had recommended,...and she was fully cured...and she lived twenty-three years after her cure."[27]

"As it was narrated to us by witnesses, he [St. Columba] healed the maladies of...sick people by the invocation of the name of Christ... For many sick persons, believing, recovered perfect health, being sprinkled with *Water blessed* by him.

"Mention has been made above of the element of water. We ought not to be silent as to other miracles with the Lord wrought through the Saint in the case of the same created thing [Sc. Blessed Water].[28]

"...And he [St. Columba] raising his holy hand with invocation of the name of Christ, washes his hands and feet [in a noxious well]. Then with his companions he drinks of the same

---

[26]St. Adamnan's *Life of St. Columba*, Book II, Chap. IV.

[27]*Ibidem*, Book II, Chap. V.

[28]St. Adamnam's *Life of St. Columba,* Book II., Chap. X.

water he had *blessed.* From that day the demons departed from that spring, and not only was it not permitted to injure anyone, but after *being blessed* by the Saint…many diseases…were cured by it."[29]

The *Book of Mulling*, a Celtic manuscript written between 650 and 750 A. D., and preserved in the library of Trinity College, Dublin, contains, among other formulae, that for the liturgical blessing of Salt and Water. Another Irish MS. known as the *St. Gall Fragments*, written about 750 A.D., and kept in the library of St. Gallen, Switzerland, has also a blessing for Salt and Water. – *"Benedictio super aquam."*[30]

Holy Water – England.

That Holy Water sprinkling was a prominent feature of the ceremonial of the Catholic Church in England before the great apostasy of the sixteenth century is evident from countless records and monuments which have come down to us. It is true that very few Holy Water stoups of the mediaeval churches have been preserved. They were walled up, or cut flush with the masonry, as the so-called reformers wished to destroy every trace and mark of the old Religion.[31]

The well-known letter of Pope St. Gregory the Great (590-604 A.D.) to St. Mellitus, whom he sent to Britain to assist St. Augustine in 601 A.D., bears out our statement.

"When… Almighty God shall bring you to the Most

---

[29]*Ibidem*, Book II., Chap. XI.

[30]Warren's *Celtic Church.*

[31]Many of these stoups, which had been filled up with mortar and stone by the vandals of the sixteenth century, have recently been brought to light by Ritualistic restorers. They are usually to be found on the outside of the main entrance to the right and fixed in the wall.

Reverend Bishop, Augustine, our brother, tell him what I have, upon mature deliberation on the affair of the English, determined upon, *viz.*, that the temples of the idols, in that nation, ought not to be destroyed. But let the idols that are in them be destroyed. Let *Holy Water* be made and sprinkled in the said temples," etc.[32]

The following incident in the life of St. Cuthbert (637-687 A.D.), as related by Ven. Bede, testifies to the use of Holy Water in the seventh century. During one of his pastoral Visitations St. Cuthbert was entertained at the house of a nobleman whose wife was lying ill and at the point of death. "May I request you," said the nobleman, "to bless water and sprinkle it upon my wife so that she may recover her health, or be released from her agony as God should please." The Saintly Bishop, complying with the request of his host, blessed water and ordered his chaplain to sprinkle it over the speechless and unconscious woman, besides giving her some Holy Water to drink. Immediately she sat up, having recovered in an instant the full use of her faculties and perfect health.[33]

The pious custom of using Holy Water is also clearly indicated in the literature of the Catholic ages. Witness, for instance, the striking passage from Chaucer's celebrated Canterbury Tales (A.D. 1340-1400).[34]

> "Upon his bierë lay this innocent
> Before the altar while Massë last;
> And, after that, the Abbot with his convent
> Have sped them for to bury him full fast;
> And when they *Holy Water* on him cast,
> Yet spake the child when *sprinkled was the water,*

---

[32]*St. Bede, Eccles. Hist.*, Book I., Chap. 27, etc.

[33]Ven. Bede. Vita S. Cuthbert, Chap. XXV.

[34]*The Princess's Tale.*

And Sang 'O Alma Redemptoris Mater.'"

Shakespeare, the great English poet and dramatist (1564-1616), makes frequent references in his works to Holy Water; for instance,[35] "I swear by all the Roman gods, since priest and *Holy Water* are so near."

> "O nuncle, Court *Holy Water* in a dry house
> Is better than this rain water out of door."[36]
> "There she shook
> The *Holy Water* from her heavenly eyes."[37]
> "… My tears that fall
> "Prove *Holy Water* on thee."[38]

The Asperges: its Institution and History.

Besides this sprinkling, the priest sprinkles the congregation at the commencement of the Holy Sacrifice – principal Mass. This latter ceremony, known as Asperges, is very ancient. Over a thousand years have elapsed since it was prescribed by the reigning Pope, St Leo IV., A.D. 847. It is mentioned in a Canon of Synod quoted by Hincmar, Archbishop of Rheims, who lived in the beginning of the ninth century; and also by Walafrid Strabo, who lived in the same century.

And although no evidence has been produced to show that this beautifully expressive rite was observed before the ninth

---

[35]Andronicus I. I. 323.

[36]King Lear, 3.2.10.

[37]*Ibidem* 4.3.32.

[38]Cymbel. 5.5.269.

century of our era – so writes Martene – there is strong ground for believing that it dates back from a far earlier age. The following are the words of the saintly Pontiff, Leo IV, bearing on this question, and addressed to the Bishops and Clergy of his day: "Every Sunday before Mass, bless water with which the people may be sprinkled, and have a vessel specially for that purpose."[39] Many writers who treat of the ancient ceremonies and usages of the early Church, maintain that these words of the Sovereign Pontiff must be considered as a direction for the strict observance of a custom already existing, rather than an introduction of a new ceremony.

And here it may be observed that, in regard to the ceremony of the Asperges before Mass, the congregation constitutes one body. Hence in order to receive the benefit of the Holy Water, and to partake of the spiritual and other blessings attached to the rite, it is not necessary that the water should fall on each individual person present; just as it is not necessary that it should fall upon every candle in the blessing given on Candlemas Day, or on each one of the palms blessed on Palm Sunday. It is sufficient that the water be sprinkled over the congregation as a whole.

Modern Liturgical Blessing of Water.

When a priest – using the liturgical prayers of the Church – consecrates water to sacred use, he first exorcises and blesses salt, then water, and mixes both in the name of the Most Holy Trinity. By such blessing the priest withdraws these substances from the power of the devil who, since the fall, has corrupted to a certain extent all animate and inanimate things. Water and salt are elements which enter largely into the constitution of all things we employ for cleanliness, health and food. Water slakes our thirst,

---

[39]Fornici, *Ed. Monast.*, 1853, p. 390.

abates the fevers of the system, is a constituent of all our foods and drinks, and is used in washing and cleansing, and so has become a fitting emblem of cleanliness of conscience and purity of soul. Salt is employed in flavoring our food, and in preserving meats and other foods from putrefaction, and hence salt is recognized as an emblem of prudence and incorruption. Hence Holy Water – a combination of both – is meant to be a symbol of purity and incorruption, of holiness and immortality; and when we enter our churches and are sprinkled with it we are thereby admonished that if we wish to be purified and preserved from the corruption and putrefaction of sin we can attain to that condition only by sanctifying Grace conveyed to us through the sacraments which the priests of the Church administer to us in the temple of the living God.

Holy Water is not Symbolical only.

Is Holy Water a mere type of purity, a mere symbol of incorruption? No. It is an indirect source of sanctification. It is an antidote against spiritual and corporal disease. An efficient remedy against evil of all kinds, provided it is used in the right spirit and with proper intention. The priests of the Church receive at their ordination power to give blessings to various things, *viz.*, palms on Palm Sunday, ashes on Ash Wednesday, candles on Candlemas Day, rosaries, scapulars, water. The faculty of bestowing such blessings does not depend on the worthiness or unworthiness of the priest. It depends on God who is the one only source of all divine blessings.

Paschal Holy Water.

But there are other uses of Holy Water at home as well as at the church. The water which is blessed before Mass on Holy

Saturday morning, and which is known as Easter Holy Water,[40] differs from ordinary Holy Water by reason of the greater solemnity and the more elaborate ritual accompanying its blessing.[41] The water is invariably blessed in the Baptistery on the occasion in question. Part of the water so blessed is intended to remain in the baptismal font to be used *exclusively* in the administration of the Sacrament of Baptism. Before the consecrated oil of Catechumens and holy Chrism are poured into the font, the celebrant takes some of the water and sprinkles himself and the congregation with it. Some more of it is taken for sprinkling in the dwellings of the faithful on Holy Saturday alone, as well as for sprinkling in the church on Easter Sunday morning before the principal Mass.

In former times it was customary for one of the priests of the parish to sprinkle the homes of his people with Holy Water on Holy Saturday morning, and though the custom still prevails in many places, it has been found impossible to observe it everywhere owing to the extent of the parish and the limited number of priests. The faithful, however, are recommended to take with them from the church a little phial of the Easter water for the sprinkling of their families and houses and belongings. But some Catholic writers maintain that it ought not to be used on other occasions, when ordinary Holy Water is prescribed, such as for the sick room, in the administration of the Sacraments, etc.

---

[40][Editor: sometimes called lustral water.]

[41]This ceremony dates back from earliest age of the Christian Era, and the formula prescribed in the ritual for blessing the water is found in the Apostolic Constitutions, and in the liturgies of the Oriental and Western Churches.

HOLY WATER

Other Blessings of Water.

Besides those above described there are several other blessings of water. Water is blessed on the eve of Pentecost, with ceremonies similar to those of Holy Saturday, for use in the administration of Baptism. It is also blessed for the following liturgical functions, *viz.*, the laying of the foundation stone of a new church, the dedication and consecration of a new church, chapel, altar, cemetery, bell, for the reconciliation or re-consecration of a church or cemetery which has been desecrated. There is a distinct formula for the blessing of water on the occasion of each of the above ceremonies. The various formulas are found in the "Ceremonial of Bishops."[42]

Holy Water in our Homes.

Every Catholic home should be provided with Holy Water at all times, and it is a painful revelation to a priest to discover on his arrival at the house of a devout (?) Catholic family, that no Holy Water is to be had in the house. He may have to administer Holy Communion to a chronic invalid, or he may be required to prepare some one in the house for death, or perform the funeral service over the remains of a deceased person. He may be called to bless a new dwelling. For all or any of these rites Holy Water is

---

[42]In the ("Orthodox") Eastern Church water is solemnly blessed by prelates or Bishops on the evening of January 5th, because they have a tradition that our Divine Lord was baptized on the following day. The people drink of this Holy Water, and sprinkle it on their houses and property. In the Armenian Church the Bishop blesses water only once a year, *viz.*, on the Feast of the Epiphany. The ceremony is known as the baptism of the Cross, because during the ceremony the Cross, which is intended for the Altar is partly immersed in the Holy Water. – Bergier, *Diction. De Theolog.*

prescribed in the liturgy of the Church.

Souls in Purgatory and Holy Water.

As the rich man, of whom Our Blessed Lord speaks to us in the Gospel, cried out when buried in hell, to Abraham on whose bosom the poor man Lazarus rested, "Father Abraham, have mercy on me, and send Lazarus that he may dip the tip of his finger in water, to cool my tongue, for I am tormented in this flame," so the poor suffering souls in purgatory cry out to us: "Ah! Christian, have pity on us: dip your fingers in the Holy Water blessed by the Church's prayers, and procure for us some little refreshment for we suffer much in these terrible flames of Purgatory."[43]

It has at all times been a praiseworthy custom adopted by the Church in her solemn ceremonies over the remains of the faithful departed, to sprinkle them with Holy Water; for as the rain falling from Heaven refreshes the flowers which have become faded by the sun's rays, so does Holy Water procure refreshment to the poor souls suffering in Purgatory, those chosen flowers of Heaven which are being burned by the sun of God's justice.

A priest who had died, appeared, soon after death, in visions to St. Martin (Canon Regular of Liege). He informed the saint that he was in purgatory and then made the following statement, "as often as the faithful sprinkle Holy Water on our graves our sufferings diminish and just as you are refreshed on earth by drinking or bathing in fresh water when you suffer from great heat, so we in purgatory are refreshed by Holy Water."[44]

---

[43]*Deodatus in Vitis Patauno.*

[44]Mendo. In append, Cruc. disp IV.

HOLY WATER

Care of Holy Water Stoups.

Holy Water, being a sacramental, something that is consecrated for use in the ceremonies and sacred rites of our holy religion, and in the service of God, it should be preserved in a manner in keeping with its sacred purpose and character. A glass-stoppered bottle or other decent receptacle should be obtained for keeping a constant supply, and the supply should be renewed frequently so as not to allow sediment to form in the bottle, from dust or other causes. Every bedroom in the house should have a small font or stoup suspended or resting on a bracket, and partially filled with Holy Water so that members of the family may sprinkle themselves with it occasionally, especially on rising from sleep and retiring to rest at night. A small sponge may be placed in the little stoup. It has the advantage of retaining the liquid and of preserving it from being spilled. If dust accumulates in the stoup, the Holy Water should be thrown into the fire or into a garden, but never into sinks or drains, and the stoup and sponge should be washed.

Holy Water should not be employed for any purpose, or in any manner, except in the spirit of the expressive solemn prayer of the liturgy used in its blessing, *viz.*, that by its efficacy and through the invocation of the Holy Spirit and the merits of Jesus Christ it may repel the evil spirit, restrain him in his attempts to injure us spiritually or otherwise; that we may be preserved from spiritual harm, and that we may secure the divine blessing in all that concerns soul and body.

Miracles performed through Holy Water.

The Church teaches that Almighty God is pleased to honor the relics of His Saints, by making their relics instruments of healing, and of other miracles, and also by bestowing spiritual favors on those who keep and respect relics. In the Old Testament, for instance, (IV. Kings xiii), relates that the sick were healed by contact with towels which had touched the living body of St. Paul.

In the Gospel of St. Mark (v. 25, *et seq*.), it is related that a woman was instantly cured of an inveterate disease of twelve years' standing by merely touching the hem of Our Divine Lord's garment, and even the shadow of St. Peter falling on the sick healed them of their diseases (Acts v., 15). The history of the Church and the lives of the Saints contain accounts of well authenticated miracles, similar to the above, wrought upon persons who were sprinkled with Holy Water. The difference between the two classes of miracles is this, that whereas the Scripture miracles were performed through the instrumentality of something that pertained to a Saint or very holy person, the latter miracles were performed through the agency of something which received the solemn blessing of the Church, *viz*., Holy Water. In both cases the Omnipotent God is the principal agent and author of the miracle. We select for insertion here a few examples of the latter class of miracle, out of many that might be given.[45]

The Blind See.

At Kiang-Si in China the son of a convert woman lost the sight of one eye. The mother was urged by her pagan neighbors to offer sacrifice to their idol, who would infallibly cure her son. The woman refused to commit so great a sin, and informed the pagans that she had boundless trust in God – the true God – to whom she would pray. Soon after this the child lost the use of his other eye, whereupon the pagans upbraided the mother for her "superstitious folly in trusting in her God." The poor distracted woman, however, only turned all the more eagerly to God, and then, as if impelled by divine inspiration, she dropped a little Holy Water upon the child's blind eyes. In an instant his sight was completely restored to him, and many of the pagans, being satisfied as to the reality of the cure,

---

[45]From Pare Rossignoli, S.J., *Merveiles Divines, Les Saints des Temps Modernes.*

declared their belief in the Catholic Faith.

The Dead Rise.

At Bumm (Province of Neau, China), a Christian woman died of malignant fever. Her son, Benedict, a devout convert to the Faith, was overwhelmed with grief because his mother died without the Sacraments. A multitude of Christians and pagans came to the funeral of the deceased who was deservedly respected by all classes. Just before the coffin was closed down Benedict begged the faithful to unite with him in prayer for his mother. Meanwhile he poured some Holy Water on the lips of the dead woman, and immediately, to the amazement of all present, she rose up alive and completely restored to health. The miracle is said to have led to the conversion of nine hundred pagans.

Demons are Expelled.

Father M. Ricci, a missioner in China, sought in Nankin a house which he could use for a chapel. Leo-Ten, the chief mandarin, offered him one. "But I warn you, Father," said Leo, "for the place is infested by evil spirits which terrify the neighborhood with their infernal shrieks and noises." Father Ricci gladly accepted the offer. He blessed the house, sprinkling every part of it with Holy Water. From that moment the demons ceased to give trouble, and the astounded pagans came eagerly to hear the missioner's instructions and soon many of them requested to be baptized.

A Spiritualistic Seance is Spoiled.

"While some of our Fathers," writes Father Muller, C.S.S.R, "were giving a mission in Erie, a meeting of spiritualists was held in that city. When the bishop heard of it, he sent one of our Fathers to prevent the evil spirits from exercising their influence over their mediums.

"The Father went in disguise to the house where the meeting was to take place. He took with him a bottle of Holy Water.

"Before the performance began the Father sprinkled the whole floor with the Holy Water. The medium, a young woman, almost immediately came upon the stage to get into a trance, but could not succeed. They tried for about an hour, but got no answer.

"At last the performer - the medium - said: 'Ladies and gentlemen, we have to give up tonight. There must be present some opposing power, as the spirits do not appear nor speak."[46]

Power of Priests to Consecrate Water to Sacred Use.

A priest duly ordained in the ministry, receives in virtue of his ordination, authority and power to bestow blessing to attach blessing. He, as the accredited agent of God, invoking a blessing in the name of God, and using a liturgical prayer attaches God's blessing to Holy Water. Hence, when we are sprinkled with Holy Water we obtain a certain blessing. We come under the influence of the prayer uttered by the priest as representative of the Church. The invocation pronounced by the priest in blessing the water, ascends anew to heaven and brings down on us – more or less according to our disposition and interior devotion – the graces and blessing implored by the Church for soul and body.

Holy Water, therefore, being one of the Sacramentals – not a Sacrament – has this special efficacy, that when we sprinkle it on ourselves, accompanying the outward act with a desire that God may cleanse our souls, the prayer of the whole Church, interceding for us is joined to our own.

St. Teresa, that renowned servant of God, so distinguished among the Saints, on account of her admirable qualities of heart

---

[46]M. Muller, *First Com.*, p. 353.

and mind, in speaking of Holy Water, says in her life, written by herself (Chapter XXXI) –

"I know by frequent experience that there is nothing which puts the devils to flight like Holy Water. They run away before the Sign of the Cross also, but they return immediately; great then must be the power of Holy Water. As for me, my soul is conscious of a special and most distinct consolation whenever I take it. Indeed I feel almost always a certain refreshing, which I cannot describe, together with an inward joy, which comforts my whole soul. This is no fancy, nor a thing that occurred only once; for it has happened very often, and I have watched it very carefully. I may compare what I feel with that which happens to a person in great heat, and very thirsty, drinking a cup of cold water – his whole being is refreshed. I consider that everything ordained by the Church is very important, and I have a joy in reflecting that the words of the Church are so mighty that they endow water with power so that there shall be so great a difference between Holy Water and water that has never been blessed."

Prayer of the Church in Blessing Water.

The following is the spirit if not the exact words of the liturgical prayer used by the Church in blessing Holy Water. "O God! The Creator of all things, Author and Source of all Grace; we humbly and suppliantly implore Thee to bless and sanctify these elements of Thy Creation – salt and water – that wheresoever, and on whomsoever they may be sprinkled Thy blessing and Divine protection may be imparted for the welfare of soul and body, in virtue of the merits of our Lord Jesus Christ, who liveth, etc."

Shall we be surprised then that Holy Water is placed at the doors of our Churches, and that we are sprinkled with it every Sunday by the Priest? Is it done to drive away the devil? Is he to be found at the foot of God's altar, at the entrance to the house of God? Yes! Sacred things are like rich treasures. Treasures attract thieves. Sacred things attract demons who try to rob us of them.

But, why Holy Water? Chiefly to dispose and prepare ourselves for reception of the Sacraments and especially for the Eucharistic Banquet to which all are invited, and of which all are supposed to partake in reality, or at least in spirit. In the days of ancient hospitality when a stranger was received by the host into his house, the feet of the guest were washed in token of friendship and charity, before he was admitted into the intimacy of the family circle. The travel-stained wayfarer had the dust and grime of the road removed from off feet and hands and garments, and so he was refreshed for the enjoyment of the hospitality of his host. Christ our Lord consecrated this beautiful custom at the Last Supper when He washed the feet of His beloved disciples. We are strangers, travelers, exiles on earth. Jesus Christ, our dear Lord, offers us the hospitality of His Sacred Temple – His Church. Hither we come for comfort, spiritual refreshment and strength. Hither we come to rest from the fatigue and weariness of the rugged road. Here He prepares His Banquet for us. Here He breaks for us the bread of friendship – the Bread of Life. "Come to Me all you that labor and are burdened, and I will refresh you." What host of ancient hospitality ever honored guest with half the welcome, half the affection with which Jesus Christ honors us? At the entrance to His house He receives us with the kiss of peace, cleanses us from the dust and grime contracted in our journey with the water into which He has put His strength and virtue, and fortifies us for the continuation and prosecution of that long journey over which we are traveling on our way to our destined home in everlasting rest with God.

Translation of the Latin Blessing of Salt and Water.

On Sundays, and whenever necessary, the priest, having prepared salt and pure water to be blessed in the church or sacristy, puts on a surplice and violet stole, and in the first place says: "Our help is in the name of the Lord, Who made heaven and earth." Then he begins the exorcism of the salt. "I exorcise thee, created substance of salt, by the living God, by the true God, by the holy God, by God, Who commanded Eliseus to cast thee into the water that it might be purified, that thou mayest become exorcised for the saving use of the faithful, that whoever use thee may enjoy health of soul and body, that all phantasms and wickedness and deceits of the devil may depart from every place where thou art sprinkled, as well as every evil spirit adjured by Him who will come to judge the living, and the dead, and the world by fire. Amen."

"Let us pray, O Almighty and Eternal God! We humbly implore Thy boundless clemency that Thou wouldst mercifully deign to bless and sanctify this salt. Thy creature, which Thou hast given for the use of mankind, that it may bring health of soul and body to all who take it, and that whatsoever is touched or sprinkled with it may be freed from all uncleanness, and from all attacks of the spirit of wickedness, through our Lord, etc."

Exorcism of the Water; the Priest says –

"I exorcise thee, created substance of water, in the name of God the Father Almighty, in the name of Jesus Christ, His Son, Our Lord, and in the power of the Holy Ghost, that thou mayest become exorcised (water) for the dispelling of all the power of the enemy of mankind and that the same enemy with his apostate angels may be expelled and routed by the power of the same Jesus Christ, our Lord, who will come to judge the living and the dead, and the world by fire. Amen."

"Let us pray, O God! Who for the salvation of mankind has wrought many great mysteries and miracles by means of the substance of water, listen propitiously to our invocations, and infuse into this element, prepared by manifold purifications, the power of Thy benediction, in order that Thy creature (water) being used as an instrument of Thy hidden works, may be efficacious in driving away devils, and curing diseases; that whatsoever in the houses or in any place of the faithful shall have been sprinkled with this water, may be freed from all uncleanliness, and delivered from all guile. Let no pestilential spirit reside there, nor infectious air. Let all snares of the hidden enemy be removed, and if there should be anything adverse to the safety or repose of the indwellers, may it be put entirely to flight by the sprinkling of this water that the welfare which we seek may, by the invocation of Thy Holy Name, be defended from all assaults, through our Lord Jesus Christ, etc."

"On Sundays, after blessing the water, the priest before he has begun the Mass sprinkles the altar (with Holy Water), then himself, and his (attendant) ministers, and finally the congregation, as the Missal prescribes. Afterwards the faithful may take away with them, in phials, some of the Holy Water for sprinkling upon their sick, and their homes, and their gardens and vineyards, *etc.*, and also for the purpose of keeping it in their rooms that they may be able to sprinkle it upon themselves every day.

Extract from letter of Pope Pius IX.

"…Considering the venerable antiquity of Holy Water, and the custom of the Church in making use of it in almost all her blessings; taking account also of its efficacy in expelling unclean spirits, and frustrating the wiles and wickedness of satanic perfidy and averting all that can be injurious to man; considering likewise the power of Holy Water in purifying the soul of lesser sins and in procuring spiritual and corporal health, – all of which should commend its urgent usefulness to the faithful, – nevertheless, it is a lamentable fact that, at a time when the necessity of such powerful succor is most pressing, the custom (of sprinkling ourselves with Holy Water) is almost everywhere neglected or at least not practiced by the majority with becoming sentiments of religion and faith.

"…It is indeed an excellent idea to remind the faithful of the sanctity, efficacy and benefits of Holy Water, holding, as it does, such high rank among the Sacramentals, so that they (the faithful)…may be instigated to use it more frequently and more religiously.... We desire earnestly to encourage and promote the use of Holy Water, even by attaching to it the benefit of indulgence." March 14, 1866

Extract from Brief of Pope Pius IX.

"Among the most ancient of the sacred rites which the Church of Jesus Christ has employed, from the beginning, in the administration of the Sacrament, instituted by Our Lord Jesus Christ, or in the sanctification of things destined for the use of the faithful, a foremost place must be given to the consecration or blessing of Water and Salt.... In blessing Water and Salt, with her prayers and invocations, the Church has the intention that God may impart to them (Water and Salt) a supernatural power of expelling evil spirits and averting diseases, and consequently that the faithful may experience salutary effects from the use of Holy Water...

"...We who ardently desire to promote Religion among the faithful and to provide for the eternal Salvation of souls, in order to make the use of Holy Water more frequent among Christians, (we) consider it expedient to open the celestial treasures of the Church ...

"Wherefore we grant ... to all the faithful who are contrite, ONE HUNDRED DAYS' INDULGENCE, each time they they make upon themselves the Sign of the Cross with Holy Water, and invoke the names of the Most Holy Trinity...applicable to the souls in Purgatory." April 25th, 1866.

APPENDIX A.

CHIEFLY FOR THE REV. CLERGY.

Miss. Rom. = Roman Missal. *Caerimon. Episc.* = Ceremonial of Bishops. *Sac. Rit. Cong.* = Sacred Congregation of Rites. *Rit. Rom.* = Roman Ritual

---

Blessing of Water.

1. Lest the Holy Water in the stoups at the church entrances, and in the ordinary vessels in the Sacristy, become corrupt or foul the *Caerimon. Episc. (Lib.* I., Cap. VI., n.2) prescribes that the water be blessed at least once every week. The frequent use made of Holy Water in ecclesiastical functions, and the custom among the faithful of carrying it home with them for sprinkling their houses, fields, etc. (*Rit. Rom.* Tit. VIII, Cap. II.) necessitates this frequent blessing.

2. In churches in which the *Asperges* takes place before the principal Mass on Sundays, the Water should be blessed every Sunday, according to the *Miss. Rom. (in fine)* in the sacristy, and according to the *Rit. Rom* (Tit. VIII., Cap. II.) in the church. Easter Sunday and Pentecost Sunday are excepted from this regulation in regard to churches which have a baptismal font, for a sufficient amount of Holy Water for the *Asperges* is taken out of the Baptismal font on the Vigils of these Sundays before the Holy Oils are mixed with it *(Miss. Rom.*)

3. If the supply of Holy Water is likely to be exhausted before the next regular blessing, ordinary water may be added in a *smaller* quantity than the residue of Holy Water. By this mixture all the water is considered *blessed*, according to the scholastic axiom *"Major pars trahit ad se minorem"* (Hartmann, 232): or water may be blessed at any time or place (Rit. Rom., Tit VIII. Cap II.).

4. If the water be blessed on Sundays by the priest who is

to give the *Asperges*, he should be vested in amice, alb, cincture, and stole (crossed on this chest), of the color of the Mass vestments (*Miss. Rom.*). If, however, the water be blessed by another priest on Sundays, or by any priest on any other occasion, he should wear a cotta and violet stole (*Rit. Rom.*)

5. The salt used at the blessing of water should be ordinary salt, *sal naturale*, such as is used for seasoning food, reduced to fine powder, clean and dry. (Baruffaldo, Tit. XLV., n. 19).

Once blessed the salt can be used on future occasions. (Sac. Rit. Cong., April 8th, 1713), when the exorcism and blessing of the salt shall be omitted.

6. When reciting the words "Commixtio salis et aquae pariter fiat in nomine Patris et Filii et Spiritus Sancti," the priest takes between his fingers, or in the palm of his right hand a small quantity of the blessed salt, which he lets fall, in a continuous course, into the water three times, in the form of a cross at the words *Patris, Filii* and *Spiritus Sancti*. A spoon or other instrument may, however, be used for dropping the salt into the water. If there are several vessels containing water to be blessed, it is sufficient to read the exorcisms and prayers once over all without any change. But the blessed salt must be dropped into each vessel and the formula "Commixtio salis, etc.," must be repeated each time.